The Obedience Of Faith
(James-Revelation)

Brother Jon

Editing by Emily Leeper

Interior Book Design by Brother Jon

Cover Design by Brother Jon

Printed in the United States of America

18

Contents

Introduction
He Who Obeys The Son

To begin this last book of the series: *The Obedience Of Faith*, I would like to look at some words of the Lord Jesus. True faith and true obedience are inseparably linked. We can have faith so as to do great spiritual things, yet if we do not obey the Lord we will not be saved. That is just what Jesus said:

> **Not everyone who says to Me, 'Lord, Lord,' will enter the kingdom of heaven, but he who does the will of My Father who is in heaven *will enter.* [n] Many will say to Me on that day, 'Lord, Lord, did we not prophesy in Your name, and in Your name cast out demons, and in Your name perform many [n]miracles?' [n] And then I will declare to them, 'I never knew you; depart from Me, you who practice lawlessness.'** (Matthew 7:21-23)

It is highly doubtful that any of us have done such great spiritual things, things that would seem to indicate a relationship with Christ. They were sure they loved Christ and were heaven bound. In the same way so many of us walk in obedience to our pleasures rather than to Christ. If this is true will not the same judgment be upon us as these experienced?

Jesus said, **"He who believes in the Son has eternal life; but he who does not obey the Son will not see life, but the wrath of God abides on him"** (John 3:36). We have so many Christians who have prayed the sinner's prayer, yet are living for this world and the things it offers; they do **"not obey**

the Son." Obedience in the Christian life does more than show we are saved; it is a necessary part of salvation. It is my contention that salvation is a partnership: Jesus saves us and we abide in Him. To abide means to obey. When these two things happen we will enter eternal glory. We can camp out at church, making it to every gathering, but if we walk in sinfulness the wrath of God abides on us.

I do hope you will join with me as we look at these very important teachings from the book of James through Revelation, and in the other books as we go through all the epistles and the book of Acts along with Revelation.

Chapter 1
A Look At James
(Part one)

As we begin our look at James we will start with a couple of very strong verses regarding obedience. James writes, **"Therefore, putting aside all filthiness and *all* that remains of wickedness"** (James 1:21a). James mentions filthiness. This, of course is moral wickedness. The Christian is to have no part in it any longer. I like what he says next, **"and *all* that remains of wickedness."** Hey, whatever is still there, abandon it. It does not matter how long we've known the Lord, or how well—think of King David with Bathsheba, and the murder of her husband—we have the potential for these things. We are to flee from them, and all that remains of them.

James continues and says, **"In humility receive the word implanted, which is able to save your souls"** (James 1:21b). To receive the Word implanted in our hearts means more than knowing them, or as many think, memorizing the Scriptures. It is taking action upon them in faith. Notice that we need to do this with humility. It is the arrogant heart that is like the hardened soil in Jesus' parable. It is the humble believer who will benefit. What is the benefit? It is **"able to save your soul."**

James goes on and writes what are some of the most important words of all the epistles, **"But prove yourselves doers of the word"** (James 1:22a). Indeed, we need to put the promises of God, and the commands of God into practice. When God's Word says set aside filthiness, we need to do so. When God's Word says don't worry, we've got to stop worrying. We need to be practitioners of the Word **"and not merely hearers who delude themselves"** (James 1:22b). When we take in the Bible on Sunday mornings or during our own study time, and we don't take obedient action we merely **"delude"** ourselves into thinking we are virtuous. Many think just being at the Bible study, or at church is the goal. It merely begins there.

A couple of verses later James continues, **"But one who looks intently at the perfect law, the *law* of liberty, and abides by it, not having become a forgetful hearer but an effectual doer, this man will be blessed in what he does"** (James 1:25). Clearly he is not talking about the Law of Moses when he speaks of the **"the perfect law, the *law* of liberty."** He is speaking of New Testament teaching. He says to look intently at it. That means more than a mere glance, hearing the preacher and forgetting about it before you hit the door. We need to spend time with it and concentrate on the teachings.

James is going to basically repeat what he said a few verses earlier (verses 21-22). This must be a *very* important point in the Christian life. He says we can't be **"a forgetful hearer."** That is, taking it lightly as if we have better things to do. No, we are to be **"an effectual doer."** We need to hear it as if our lives depended upon it, and put the things we read and hear into practice. Next he adds something not mentioned in the previous verses. He says the one who obeys the Word of God, **"will be blessed in what he does."** Do you want to be blessed by God in your life? We all do. Then we need to *apply* the Word of God to our lives. We can begin with this book.

Chapter 2
A Look At James
(Part two)

Often in Christian circles the term "religion" is used in a bad light as it is used to speak of a false Christianity, one not based on a true relationship with Christ. Here James will use it to speak of true Christianity. He says, **"Pure and undefiled religion in the sight of** *our* **God and Father is this: to visit orphans and widows in their distress,** *and* **to keep oneself unstained by the world"** (James 1:27). I suppose widows and particularly orphans are in the greatest **distress**, as he put it. I must admit to my shame I have no involvement with widows or orphans beyond the orphanage in Guatemala I give to at church. I need to look more into this. James adds to this with these words, **"*and* to keep oneself unstained by the world."** This is something I am doing better at. Personally I think it is the more important point. As Christians we are so often very caught up in the world, living and thinking like the lost around us. Many are stained by the world.

Going on to chapter two verse fourteen, James says, **"What use is it, my brethren, if someone says he has faith but he has no works? Can that faith save him?"** Who in our churches (and many who never darken a door of a church) doesn't say they have faith in God? Yet their lives, year after year, remain unchanged! James asks a very important question here. What use is this kind of faith? I would have to assume it is useless. To this James has another important question. He asks, **"Can that faith save him?"** I would have to assume it can't.

A few verses later James is continuing with this same line of thought and he writes, **"But someone may *well* say, "You have faith and I have works; show me your faith without the works, and I will show you my faith by my works"** (James 2:18). James is not talking about earning our salvation. He is talking about true redemption. Salvation is a partnership between us and God, one where we are doers of the Word and show the fruit of it. It is the one who lives an obedient life, in humility before God's Word, who God will receive unto Himself. This is the faith that saves, as James mentions in verse fourteen.

Going on a couple of verses further he writes in James 2:20, **"But are you willing to recognize, you foolish fellow, that faith without works is useless?"** It is interesting that James refers to those who call themselves Christians, but have no change in their lives, **"foolish."** It is foolhardy to expect to stand before the infinitely holy God of all Creation with a faith that couldn't produce any transformation. He says a faith without godly works is **"useless."** Jesus talked about the same thing when He said, **"You are the salt of the earth; but if the salt has become tasteless, how can it be made salty *again*? It is no longer good for anything, except to be thrown out and trampled underfoot by men"** (Matthew 5:13).

Continuing he writes in the next two verses: **"Was not Abraham our father justified by works when he offered up Isaac his son on the altar? ²² You see that faith was working with his works, and as a result of the works, faith was perfected"** (James 2:21-22). Do you have a lifeless faith? Repent and humbly follow God's Word in obedience. Faith must be lived out in our lives as the first two books in this series clearly show. James says here that as a result of

Abraham putting his faith into action (**"works"**) his **"faith was perfected."**

Countless numbers around our nation have prayed the sinners prayer and are sure they have faith in God (Why else would they be in church?), yet don't have the fruit of a changed life. James plainly and succinctly says, **"You see that a man is justified by works and not by faith alone"** (James 2:24). He gives another example to win over his audience in verse twenty-five: **"In the same way, was not Rahab the harlot also justified by works when she received the messengers and sent them out by another way?"** It wasn't enough for her to be in awe of the God of Israel, which she clearly was, she had to take action. That action meant risking her own life to assist the two spies. James has one more illustration as he says, **"For just as the body without *the* spirit is dead, so also faith without works is dead"** (James 2:26). Do you have a changed life for Christ? Or are you among the living dead?

Chapter 3
A Look At James
(Part three)

Let's begin our look at James chapter three. James has a question I like very much. He asks at the beginning of verse thirteen, **"Who among you is wise and understanding?"** We all want to think that we are counted among those considered wise, but generally we think of those people who have special understanding or insight into life, or the Scriptures as being wise. Let's look though at what James says, **"Let him show by his good behavior his deeds in the gentleness of wisdom"** (James 3:13b). He says the wise man or the woman of understanding are the ones who have a life of good behavior; it is the one with deeds of gentleness that truly has **"wisdom."**

In the very next verse he comes from the opposite direction: **"But if you have bitter jealousy and selfish ambition in your heart, do not be arrogant and *so* lie against the truth"** (James 3:14). The one generally thought of as wise and insightful can have self-serving goals, or arrogance. We are not to think this one is wise. As I write this we are in the beginnings of Primary Season for Presidential candidates; this verse speaks volumes for many of the candidates.

Let's go to chapter four and see what else James has to say about obedience:

You adulteresses, do you not know that friendship with the world is hostility toward God? Therefore whoever wishes to be a friend of the world makes

himself an enemy of God. [5] Or do you think that the Scripture speaks to no purpose: "He jealously desires the Spirit which He has made to dwell in us"? (James 4:4-5)

He begins here with a scorching expression: **"You adulteresses!"** Wow! He is obviously talking to believers, and he says they are committing adultery against God. Why does he make this inflammatory statement? He tells us next that it is because rather than pursuing a friendship with God they have a **"friendship with the world."** Countless numbers among us likely have a great bond with this life; maybe we ourselves. Most of us don't realize it is such a serious matter. It is.

James goes on with another strong word saying it is **"hostility toward God."** When believers can't talk about anything beyond their weekend fun, the latest gossip, or their worldly plans for the future, it is not a good sign. On the heels of this James says, **"Therefore whoever wishes to be a friend of the world makes himself an enemy of God."** Hostility toward God was bad enough, but he says that by this the believer makes himself **"an enemy of God."** Can a true believer become God's enemy? James apparently thought so. He would know better than you or me. James finishes up these verses by saying, **"[God] jealously desires the Spirit which He has made to dwell in us."** I take this to mean He wants the Holy Spirit to have His way in our lives, that is, control us to bear the fruit of the Spirit.

Two verses later he writes, **"Submit therefore to God"** (James 4:7a). We need to walk in obedience, plain and simple. We need to resist temptation, plain and simple. Look what James says next, **"Resist the devil and he will flee from you"** (James 4:7b). Too many times, countless times, we have believed Satan rather than God; we have believed the temptations to sin are too great for us or the end result is too sumptuous to resist. Lies! Our Creator says if we resist, Satan will flee. James continues, **"Draw near to God and He will draw near to you"** (James 4:8a). What a grand and absolutely wonderful promise from a faithful God! We often pray for God to be near to us, and at the same time we refuse with our choices to draw near to Him. What are we to do? James says it is simple, **"Cleanse your hands, you sinners; and purify your hearts, you double-minded"** (James 4:8b). We need to turn from sin and walk in obedience.

What about those who have turned from God? James tells us in chapter five: **"My brethren, if any among you strays from the truth and one turns him back, ²⁰ let him know that he who turns a sinner from the error of his way will save his soul from death and will cover a multitude of sins"** (James 5:19-20). Some students of the Word are sure James is talking about fake Christians, but he talks about turning him **"back."** How can you turn a fake Christian back to Christ? No, James is talking about true Christians. What happens when we turn the wayward believer back to Christ? Two things: One, we **"save his soul from death."** That is very serious. Two, we **"will cover a multitude of sins."** The believer will find the necessary and complete cleansing of his sins in Christ.

Chapter 4
A Look At First Peter
(Part one)

Let's begin our look at First Peter and see what he has to say about obedience. He writes, **"[To those who are chosen] according to the foreknowledge of God the Father, by the sanctifying work of the Spirit, to obey Jesus Christ and be sprinkled with His blood: May grace and peace be yours in the fullest measure"** (1 Peter 1:2). Why has God **"chosen"** us? That we would obey Jesus Christ. This is this whole book in a nutshell. God didn't primarily save us to get to heaven. We should see that as a bonus; He primarily saved us to live for Him.

Peter will continue talking about our great salvation several verses later:

Therefore, prepare your minds for action, keep sober *in spirit*, fix your hope completely on the grace to be brought to you at the revelation of Jesus Christ.[14] As obedient children, do not be conformed to the former lusts *which were yours* in your ignorance, [15] but like the Holy One who called you, be holy yourselves also in all *your* behavior; [16] because it is written, "You shall be holy, for I am holy." [17] If you address as Father the One who impartially judges according to each one's work, conduct yourselves in fear during the time of your stay *on earth*; [18] knowing that you were not redeemed with perishable things like silver or gold from your futile way of life inherited from your forefathers, [19] but with

precious blood, as of a lamb unblemished and spotless, *the blood* of Christ. (1 Peter 1:13-19)

He says to live the Christian life properly we need to **"prepare [our] minds for action."** As has been said, the Christian life is a very serious matter. We need to be prepared for it, and this begins in the mind. It is here the battle is often won or lost even before we begin. Next he says, **"Keep sober *in spirit.*"** In our spirits we are to be clear-headed. Sin clouds the mind, and our spirits then are not right. At the end of verse thirteen he says, **"Fix your hope completely on the grace to be brought to you at the revelation of Jesus Christ."** Our hope can't be in that raise we are hoping for, or in our drive to succeed in life. If we are to be successful Christians our hope needs to be on God's grace, His unmerited favor. God's grace, or His favor, is found in Christ, and it will be lavished on us without end when Christ Jesus returns for us.

He says, **"As obedient children, do not be conformed to the former lusts *which were yours* in your ignorance"** (1 Peter 1:14). We can be conformed to those things as believers and we often are. We need to turn from them as we walk in obedience. They need to be *former* lusts and not present lusts. We were ignorant before, but now the truth has set us free. We need to live accordingly. Peter goes on to say, **"like the Holy One who called you, be holy yourselves also in all *your* behavior; ¹⁶ because it is written, 'You shall be holy, for I am holy'"** (1 Peter 1:17). We are children of God, and just as our parents wanted us to obey them so our Heavenly Father wants us to be obedient. He longs for us to share in His holiness so that we can know Him intimately, and experience the abundant life Jesus came to give.

We call God our Father, and He is, praise to His Name, but Peter will mention something that should go right along with this. He says, **"If you address as Father the One who impartially judges according to each one's work conduct yourselves in fear during the time of your stay *on earth*"** (1 Peter 1:17). We often excuse our own sin while we point a finger at the next person. God won't do that; He is the impartial judge. He will not give us a break while holding the next person's feet to the fire. We need to fear God's just judgment.

God will hold each of us accountable not only because He is holy and righteous, but because of how much was paid for our redemption. Peter said we need to conduct ourselves in fear **"knowing that you were not redeemed with perishable things like silver or gold from your futile way of life inherited from your forefathers"** (1 Peter 1:18). As we know God didn't buy us out of our sinful condition with the things of this earth, **"but with precious blood, as of a lamb unblemished and spotless, *the blood* of Christ"** (1 Peter 1:19). God the Son became a man to be the sacrifice for our sin; He is the Lamb of God!

Chapter 5
A Look At First Peter
(Part two)

As we continue our look at First Peter we will see a well-known verse that I don't think has been given enough attention. **"Since you have in obedience to the truth purified your souls for a sincere love of the brethren, fervently love one another from the heart."** (1 Peter 1:22). Notice that they, themselves, had purified their own souls **"for a sincere love of the brethren."** And you thought Jesus did all the purifying? Well, me too, but we see here they did it. How? Through their **"obedience to the truth."** It would appear that our obedience has a cleansing effect on our lives. As a result of this purification they were to **"fervently love one another from the heart."** Peter goes on and says, **"for you have been born again not of seed which is perishable but imperishable,** *that is,* **through the living and enduring word of God"** (1 Peter 1:23).

Peter finishes chapter one with strong statements about Word of God which we have received, and he begins chapter two with the response we are to have to it. He says because of this great salvation we are to be **"putting aside all malice and all deceit and hypocrisy and envy and all slander"** (1 Peter 2:1). If hatred and spite, or deceitfulness has any part in our lives we are to put them aside. He also mentions hypocrisy which, as Christians, we certainly don't want. He adds envying of others or their belongings, and speaking in ways that bring harm to others. All these we are to set aside out of our lives, and **"like newborn babies, long for the pure milk of the word."** (1 Peter 2:2a). I haven't been around a newborn in a long time, but you never forget how boisterous they can be when it comes to feeding time. We are to have this same thirst for God's Word **"so that by it [we] may grow in respect to salvation."** (1 Peter 2:2b). We aren't going to grow in Christ's likeness apart from taking in the Word and acting upon it. He adds, **"If you have tasted the kindness of the Lord"** (1 Peter 2:3). If we have come to Christ we need to do this.

A little further in chapter two Peter refers to believers as aliens and strangers. Here are his words:

> **Beloved, I urge you as aliens and strangers to abstain from fleshly lusts which wage war against the soul. [12] Keep your behavior excellent among the Gentiles, so that in the thing in which they slander you as evildoers, they may because of your good deeds, as they observe *them*, glorify God in the day of visitation.** (1 Peter 2:11-12)

First of all, he calls his readers **"beloved."** By God's working, and his obedience to God's command to love one another, Peter saw them as beloved. He says, **"Beloved, I urge you as aliens and strangers to abstain from fleshly lusts which wage war against the soul"** (1 Peter 2:11). We are no longer of the world. When we lived like the world in our lost state, we were right at home. Now, we are **"aliens and strangers."** Heaven is our home, and we are to long for it, and the best way to show this longing is by **"abstain[ing] from fleshly lusts which wage war against the soul."** As we saw before it begins in the mind; we need to remember God's promises of victory and His promise of an eternal future with Him. Then we need to go out and obey, putting to death those things that war against our souls.

Peter continues, **"Keep your behavior excellent among the Gentiles"** (1 Peter 2:12a). Generally Gentiles are non-Jews, but as in many places it is used here to speak of non-Christian Gentiles. We are to be **"excellent"** in our behavior around them—excellent. Why are we to live exceptional lives around the lost? **"So that in the thing in which they slander you as evildoers, they may because of your good deeds, as they observe *them*, glorify God in the day of visitation"** (1 Peter 2:12b). When they lie about us, as they did of our Lord, they will see our goodness in living and will **"glorify God in the day of visitation."** They can say all sorts of things now, but when they are standing before God in the judgment they will be compelled to worship Him for His grace in our lives.

Chapter 6
A Look At First Peter
(Part three)

As we carry on our look at First Peter let us continue in chapter two. There he writes, **"He Himself bore our sins in His body on the cross"** (1 Peter 2:24a). Jesus died in our place. Was this solely, or primarily to get us to heaven? No, as we saw back in chapter four it is first of all that we would live holy lives. Just as Peter says here it was **"so that we might die to sin and live to righteousness"** (1 Peter 2:24b). We have been redeemed to rescue us from living our lives sinfully. We are to die to sin and live righteously.

The very next words of Peter are some of the most abused words of the epistles. They are constantly being taken out of their context. Here are the words, **"for by His wounds you were healed"** (1 Peter 2:24c). Peter has been talking about Jesus dying for us and our need to, therefore, turn from sin. Peter isn't talking about healing us from whatever might be ailing us as the verse is often used for; he is talking about a spiritual healing from sin…so that we might not live in it. He continues: **"For you were continually straying like sheep"** (1 Peter 2:25a). That we were. **"But now you have returned to the Shepherd and Guardian of your souls"** (1 Peter 2:25b). Praise to God, that though his readers were previously straying from Christ, they returned.

As we get into First Peter three we will find Peter beginning with the husband wife relationship. Here he says, **"In the same way, you wives, be submissive to your own husbands so that even if any *of them* are disobedient to the word, they may be won without a word by the behavior of**

their wives" (1 Peter 3:1). The Christian wife is to live obediently. I know this is unpopular, but it is true. Please notice that as she is submitting to God and her husband that her unbelieving husband may get saved! How? Without even a word, but through watching her life. Peter goes on and says, **"As they observe your chaste and respectful behavior"** (1 Peter 3:2). Praise to God!

Continuing several verses later Peter will talk about those who desire good days:

> **For, "The one who desires life, to love and see good days, must keep his tongue from evil and his lips from speaking deceit. [11] He must turn away from evil and do good; he must seek peace and pursue it. [12] For the eyes of the Lord are toward the righteous, and His ears attend to their prayer, but the face of the Lord is against those who do evil."** (1 Peter 3:10-12)

He is addressing **"The one who desires life, to love and see good days"** (1 Peter 3:10a). Well, that would be all of us. The world says it is attained by grabbing for all the gusto. What does Peter say needs to be done to get it? The one who really wants life **"must keep his tongue from evil and his lips from speaking deceit"** (1 Peter 3:10b). If we want life indeed we need to turn from speaking wicked things; we need to keep from speaking treacherous words.

It is not just our tongue that we need to watch over, but our life as a whole. Peter continues, **"He must turn away from evil and do good; he must seek peace and pursue it"** (1 Peter 3:11a). We are seeing that if we want the best out of life Peter says we need to obey; we need to pursue peace with

God and with our fellow man. Why? **"For the eyes of the Lord are toward the righteous, and His ears attend to their prayer"** (1 Peter 3:12a). If we turn from evil God will look lovingly upon us, and He will here our prayers. Many think God just hears our prayers because we are Christians, but that doesn't seem to be the case. Peter goes on and says, **"But the face of the Lord is against those who do evil."** (1 Peter 3:12b). Remember, this was written for Christians, not the unbelieving. If we have turned from the Lord and walk in disobedience God turns His face from us. How sad for us.

A couple of verses later Peter will talk about God's protection in the Christian life. Then he says, **"But sanctify Christ as Lord in your hearts"** (1 Peter 3:15a). To sanctify means to set apart; just as your good china is set apart for those special occasions. He adds, **"Always *being* ready to make a defense to everyone who asks you to give an account for the hope that is in you"** (1 Peter 3:15b). We need to be ready with an answer when asked about our hope in Christ, and we are to answer, not with a superior attitude, but **"with gentleness and reverence"** (1 Peter 3:15c).

Chapter 7
A Look At First Peter
(Part four)

As we continue our look at First Peter we will start chapter four:

Therefore, since Christ has suffered in the flesh, arm yourselves also with the same purpose, because he who has suffered in the flesh has ceased from sin, [2] so as to live the rest of the time in the flesh no longer for the lusts of men, but for the will of God. [3] For the time already past is sufficient *for you* to have carried out the desire of the Gentiles, having pursued a course of sensuality, lusts, drunkenness, carousing, drinking parties and abominable idolatries. (1 Peter 4:1-3)

Peter tells us we are to have the same attitude and purpose as the Lord Jesus: **"Therefore, since Christ has suffered in the flesh, arm yourselves also with the same purpose, because he who has suffered in the flesh has ceased from sin"** (1 Peter 4:1). Jesus continually died to Himself that He might live for the Father—ultimately giving His life on the cross. We are to have the same obedient goal. We have died with Christ (Romans 6:8), and as we actually apply this in our daily living we will die to sin; he who has died **"has ceased from sin."** The mature Christian can be free from sin. That is my goal and I am sure it is yours.

Peter continues, **"So as to live the rest of the time in the flesh no longer for the lusts of men, but for the will of**

God" (1 Peter 4:2). Before redemption it was our goal to serve ourselves, which we did. Now, by God's grace, it is our goal (or should be) to live for **"the will of God."** We are to no longer pursue sinful habits. **"For the time already past is sufficient *for you* to have carried out the desire of the Gentiles"** (1 Peter 4:3a). We had our day of sinful living, and we are to longer live in this way; that should be our past. Peter says, **"Having pursued a course of sensuality, lusts, drunkenness, carousing, drinking parties and abominable idolatries"** (1 Peter 4:3b). For the Christian with his head on straight those things are a source of embarrassment, and are to be avoided.

Several verses later Peter starts talking about the judgment to come. He says:

> For *it is* time for judgment to begin with the household of God; and if *it begins* with us first, what *will be* the outcome for those who do not obey the gospel of God? [18] And if it is with difficulty that the righteous is saved, what will become of the godless man and the sinner? [19] Therefore, those also who suffer according to the will of God shall entrust their souls to a faithful Creator in doing what is right. (1 Peter 4:17-19)

Peter tells us the first judgment to come will be for believers, and if God is going to rigorously judge His own children how will He not do more so to the lost. There is an interesting phrase that Peter uses: **"And if it is with difficulty that the righteous is saved"** (1 Peter 4:18a). I believe the Scriptures teach two things in regard to this statement. One, the Son of

God had to become a man and die for us; that makes being saved a **"difficult"** task. Two, salvation is a partnership in which we have a part to play; we need to abide in Christ or we won't be saved; this too makes it a difficult task, that is, to save the righteous. Peter continues, **"Therefore, those also who suffer according to the will of God shall entrust their souls to a faithful Creator in doing what is right"** (1 Peter 4:19). When we suffer for Christ we need to trust God and walk in obedience. We aren't to use it to pout and whine, or to turn to other fleshly responses.

Chapter 8
A Look At Second Peter
(Part one)

As we begin our look at Second Peter we find Peter talking about God's divine power and His Word. Peter continues:

For by these He has granted to us His precious and magnificent promises, so that by them you may become partakers of *the* divine nature, having escaped the corruption that is in the world by lust. [5] Now for this very reason also, applying all diligence, in your faith supply moral excellence, and in *your* moral excellence, knowledge, [6] and in *your* knowledge, self-control, and in *your* self-control, perseverance, and in *your* perseverance, godliness, [7] and in *your* godliness, brotherly kindness, and in *your* brotherly kindness, love. [8] For if these *qualities* are yours and are increasing, they render you neither useless nor unfruitful in the true knowledge of our Lord Jesus Christ. [9] For he who lacks these *qualities* is blind *or* short-sighted, having forgotten *his* purification from his former sins. [10] Therefore, brethren, be all the more diligent to make certain about His calling and choosing you; for as long as you practice these things, you will never stumble; [11] for in this way the entrance into the eternal kingdom of our Lord and Savior Jesus Christ will be abundantly supplied to you. (2 Peter 1:4-11)

"Now for this very reason also, applying all diligence, in your faith supply moral excellence" (2 Peter 1:5a). Peter is going to go on to talk about things to be persistently sought after. He doesn't say, "Oh, and if you get around to it...." He says, **"Applying all diligence"** we are to seek these qualities. The first mentioned is **"moral excellence."** We are to be virtuous, no, virtuous with distinction.

We are not to stop there, but to this we are to add, **"knowledge."** I am sure you would agree he is not talking about math or science, but knowledge of the things of God. We are never to quit learning spiritual things. To this we are to add **"self-control."** This came to my mind the other day: *self*-control is a fruit of the *Spirit's* control (Galatians 5:23). This is without a doubt one of the most important things on Peter's list. To this we are to add **"perseverance."** Again, this is so important, and something I don't think we do well at today with the easy lives we live.

To perseverance we are to add another important quality (though they all are important) and that is **"godliness."** We are to be like our Father in heaven. To this we are to add **"brotherly kindness."** We need so much to have this as we deal with one another here in this life. To this we are to add **"love."** Paul wrote, **"But now faith, hope, love, abide these three; but the greatest of these is love"** (1 Corinthians 13:13). Love must be the hallmark of our lives. Paul also wrote, **"Let all that you do be done in love"** (1 Corinthians 16:14). This is easier said than done.

After this amazing list Peter added, **"For if these *qualities* are yours and are increasing, they render you neither useless nor unfruitful in the true knowledge of**

our Lord Jesus Christ" (2 Peter 1:8). We need to add these qualities and grow in them or we will be **"useless nor unfruitful"** in God's hands. Peter wanted to pound this point home so he added, **"For he who lacks these** *qualities* **is blind** *or* **short-sighted,   having forgotten** *his* **purification from his former sins"** (2 Peter 1:9). **"Blind** *or* **short-sighted;"** I think the blind are those who are in deep sin in their lives, and those who are short-sighted are true believers who have fallen asleep at the wheel. He is talking about true believers because he says it is this person who has **"forgotten** *his* **purification from his former sins."**

Peter goes on to say, **"Therefore, brethren, be all the more diligent to make certain about His calling and choosing you"** (2 Peter 1:10a). This is interesting. We are to be **"all the more diligent"** to make certain that we are saved! That is what he says: **"make certain about His calling and choosing you."** How do we make certain we are saved? By the fact that we prayed a prayer years ago? No. By obedience; by adding those things he listed to our faith and continually growing in them.

Amazingly, Peter is not finished. He says, **"For as long as you practice these things, you will never stumble"** (2 Peter 1:10b). In my opinion there are two parts to this. One, it is talking about daily keeping us from individual sins, that is, from sinning at all. Jesus is able to do this! Two, a stumbling out of the Christian life. We would do this by not abiding in Christ and the Vine dresser (God the Father) would remove us from the Vine (Christ). We see this taught in John fifteen. Jesus is able to keep us from stumbling either way. Peter goes on to say, **"For in this way the entrance into the**

eternal kingdom of our Lord and Savior Jesus Christ will be abundantly supplied to you" (2 Peter 1:11). If we diligently add and grow in those things he mentioned we will have a grand introduction into heaven. We will have a magnificent entrance, a rich welcome into glory. Is this what you want? Me too. Let's be obedient.

Chapter 9
A Look At Second Peter
(Part two)

Let's continue our look at Second Peter. Writing about the Lord Jesus he says, **"For when He received honor and glory from God the Father, such an utterance as this was made to Him by the Majestic Glory, 'This is My beloved Son with whom I am well-pleased'"** (2 Peter 1:17). Peter is speaking of the transfiguration which he witnessed. God the Father spoke out of heaven and said He was **"well-pleased"** with Jesus. Was He delighted in the fact that He was His Son? No, God was pleased in Him because Jesus always walked in His will; Jesus said, **"He who sent Me is with Me; He has not left Me alone, for I always do the things that are pleasing to Him"** John 8:29).

Peter is quickly going to turn to the deceitful teachers who offered a false hope of freedom. He says:

Promising them freedom while they themselves are slaves of corruption; for by what a man is overcome, by this he is enslaved.[20] For if, after they have escaped the defilements of the world by the knowledge of the Lord and Savior Jesus Christ, they are again entangled in them and are overcome, the last state has become worse for them than the first. [21] For it would be better for them not to have known the way of righteousness, than having known it, to turn away from the holy commandment handed on to them. [22] It has happened to them according to the true proverb, "A dog returns to its own vomit," and, "A sow,

after washing, *returns* to wallowing in the mire."
(2 Peter 2:19-22)

Peter spends most of his time talking about believers who get caught in their snare. He says, **"For if, after they have escaped the defilements of the world by the knowledge of the Lord and Savior Jesus Christ."** This means they got saved. **"[And] they are again entangled in them and are overcome, the last state has become worse for them than the first"** (2 Peter 2:20). He is talking about returning to our old sins and taking on our old lives. We need to persistently watch out for this.

Peter continues, **"For it would be better for them not to have known the way of righteousness, than having known it, to turn away from the holy commandment handed on to them"** (2 Peter 2:21). This is pretty serious business! Again, we need to diligently watch out so this doesn't become our state. He continues, **"It has happened to them according to the true proverb, "A dog returns to its own vomit," and, "A sow, after washing, *returns* to wallowing in the mire"** (2 Peter 2:22). We can't let these proverbs be said of our lives, brothers and sisters.

Let's go on to chapter three where Peter says, **"Since all these things are to be destroyed in this way, what sort of people ought you to be in holy conduct and godliness"** (2 Peter 3:11). He is talking about the world we live in. *All* will be destroyed with intense burning. Therefore, how then should we live? With **"holy conduct and godliness."** Is obedience important? Oh, yeah. A couple of verses later he says, **"But according to His promise we are looking for new heavens** and a new earth, in which righteousness dwells. **Therefore, beloved, since you look for these things, be diligent to be found by Him in peace, spotless and blameless"** (2 Peter 3:14). We have a promise of an eternal existence on a new and perfect planet. How then should we live? He tells us, **"be diligent to be found by Him in peace, spotless and blameless."** That is an amazingly high calling…one which we can all reach. Praise to God.

Chapter 10
A Look At First John
(Part one)

John says these famous words in chapter one, **"This is the message we have heard from Him and announce to you, that God is Light, and in Him there is no darkness at all"** (1 John 1:5). Then he goes on to write:

> If we say that we have fellowship with Him and *yet* walk in the darkness, we lie and do not practice the truth; [7] but if we walk in the Light as He Himself is in the Light, we have fellowship with one another, and the blood of Jesus His Son cleanses us from all sin. [8] If we say that we have no sin, we are deceiving ourselves and the truth is not in us. [9] If we confess our sins, He is faithful and righteous to forgive us our sins and to cleanse us from all unrighteousness. (1 John 1:6-9)

God is spoken of as light; the darkness is all that is opposed to Him, though John speaks here of our sin. He says, **"If we say that we have fellowship with Him and *yet* walk in the darkness, we lie and do not practice the truth"** (1 John 1:6). If a sinful lifestyle is our practice and we lead others to believe we are buddy-buddy with God then we are liars. The life of a true Christian is to be lived fighting temptation not giving in to it.

John says, **"But if we walk in the Light as He Himself is in the Light, we have fellowship with one another"** (1 John 1:7a). If we turn from sin we will have true fellowship with other Christians who are doing likewise. This isn't talking about being sinless, though that is our goal, but living honestly before God. John says if we do this **"the blood of Jesus His Son cleanses us from all sin"** (1 John 1:7b). Most of us thought the blood of Christ did all its work at the cross, but in reality it is still doing its work. John continues, **"If we confess our sins, He is faithful and righteous to forgive us our sins and to cleanse us from all unrighteousness"** (1 John 1:9). Still, after conversion, we need the blood of Christ; we still need forgiveness. I had been lead to believe all my sins (past, present, and future) were forgiven at the time of conversion. That doesn't appear true. It would seem that if we don't confess our sins we will not be forgiven for sins we commit.

John begins chapter two with these words, **"My little children, I am writing these things to you so that you may not sin. And if anyone sins, we have an Advocate with the Father, Jesus Christ the righteous"** (1 John 2:1). John is very concerned about sin and he reminds us here that Jesus is our **"Advocate;"** He comes along side us and defends us. He does this while Satan accuses us (Revelation 12:10).

A couple of verses later John says, **"By this we know that we have come to know Him, if we keep His commandments"** (1 John 2:3). Again, it is not the fact that we prayed a prayer; we can have confidence before God *only* if we are walking in obedience. He says, **"The one who says, 'I have come to know Him,' and does not keep His commandments, is a liar, and the truth is not in him"** (1 John 2:4). Clearly, the many who base their salvation on a prayer with no change of their lives, as John put it, are **"liars."**

John shifts from those who don't walk in obedience to those who do and he says, **"But whoever keeps His word, in him the love of God has truly been perfected. By this we know that we are in Him"** (1 John 2:5). The one who walks in obedience, or **"keeps [God's] word"** this one, **"has truly been perfected."** We are to be perfect as our heavenly Father is perfect (Matthew 5:48). Therefore, by our obedience we do our part in salvation; not the saving itself, but the working out of our salvation (Philippians 2:12); Jesus called this abiding in Him (John 15:4).

In the next verse John says, **"The one who says he abides in Him ought himself to walk in the same manner as He walked"** (1 John 2:6). We are to live as Jesus lived. Several verses later John writes, **"The world is passing away, and *also* its lusts; but the one who does the will of God lives forever"** (1 John 2:17). We don't have to pass away as this world will; if we walk with God we can have the confidence we won't.

Chapter 11
A Look At First John
(Part two)

Salvation is a partnership between us and God; He saves us through Christ, and we on our part need to abide in Christ. John says this, **"Now, little children, abide in Him, so that when He appears, we may have confidence and not shrink away from Him in shame at His coming"** (1 John 2:28). This would be terrible! A Christian having to fall back in shame of the way they lived at the appearance of our Lord! To prevent such an occurrence we need to abide, that is, obey the Lord. In the next verse John says, **"If you know that He is righteous, you know that everyone also who practices righteousness is born of Him"** (1 John 2:29). Once again I will ask, do we know we are born of God because we prayed a prayer? No, we can only know if we are walking in obedience to Him.

In his next chapter John says:

No one who abides in Him sins; no one who sins has seen Him or knows Him. [7] Little children, make sure no one deceives you; the one who practices righteousness is righteous, just as He is righteous; [8] the one who practices sin is of the devil; for the devil has sinned from the beginning. The Son of God appeared for this purpose, to destroy the works of the devil. [9] No one who is born of God practices sin, because His seed abides in him; and he cannot sin, because he is born of God. [10] By this the children of God and the children of the devil are obvious: anyone who

does not practice righteousness is not of God, nor the one who does not love his brother. (1 John 3:6-10)

We have here several very strong statements that might not be straight forward. The first: **"No one who abides in Him sins"** (1 John 3:6a). The word **"abide"** means to abide permanently. We could think of it like this. You abide, or have permanent residence, at your house. A dinner guest is their just for a short time, though maybe many times; he does not abide there. Therefore, if we are continuing in abiding in Christ we will not walk in sin. He adds, **"no one who sins has seen Him or knows Him"** (1 John 3:6b). Well, if this were to be taken at face value we would all be excluded, including John himself. I understand this to mean, not a single sin, but the continuation in sin—a sinful lifestyle.

Next John says, **"Little children, make sure no one deceives you; the one who practices righteousness is righteous, just as He is righteous"** (1 John 3:6-10). No one can live a holy life apart from the work of Christ, though there are people like Gandhi for instance who appear to. We can know that those who really do are righteous because God is their Father. On the other hand, **"the one who practices sin is of the devil; for the devil has sinned from the beginning"** (1 John 3:8a). Those, whether in church or out, who have a lifestyle of sin are probably children of the devil. John goes on to say, **"The Son of God appeared for this purpose, to destroy the works of the devil"** (1 John 3:8b). God wants us to have the joy of sharing in His holiness, and that only comes through abiding in Christ.

The things John wrote I can pretty well navigate through, but this next statement gives me some difficulty. He says, **"No one who is born of God practices sin, because His seed abides in him; and he cannot sin, because he is born of God"** (1 John 3:9). I not only know a number of Christians who have practiced sin, I myself have; so this puzzles me. Whatever the case we can see that obedience is of utmost importance in the Christian life. John continues, **"By this the children of God and the children of the devil are obvious: anyone who does not practice righteousness is not of God, nor the one who does not love his brother"** (1 John 3:10). As a general principle this is true; those in churches who live like the devil on Saturday and appear as angels on Sunday are not of God. To this John adds that those who do not love are of the devil as well.

Chapter 12
A Look At First John
(Part three)

John mentioned love in the last verse we looked at; he will continue a few verses later by saying in 1 John 3:17, **"But whoever has the world's goods, and sees his brother in need and closes his heart against him, how does the love of God abide in him?"** We cannot be so focused on our situations that we cannot see the situations of others; if we do we likely will not be willing to help with a need even if we see it. We have to show our love, not just feel it. This is what John says next. **"Little children, let us not love with word or with tongue, but in deed and truth."** (1 John 3:18). Showing love is another form of obedience. We need to walk in love.

Do you want to have a confidence before God? I'm sure you do. John tells us how to have it. He says, **"Beloved, if our heart does not condemn us, we have confidence before God"** (1 John 3:21). We cannot have hidden sin, or outward sin for that matter. We need to walk in obedience. John will go on to say that obedience is tied to answered prayer as well. Here are his words, **"and whatever we ask we receive from Him, because we keep His commandments and do the things that are pleasing in His sight."** (1 John 3:22). We can experience answered prayer if we obey God and **"do the things that are pleasing in His sight."**

A couple of verses later he writes, **"The one who keeps His commandments abides in Him, and He in him. We know by this that He abides in us, by the Spirit whom He has given us"** (1 John 3:24). As I said in the last chapter the word **"abide"** means to abide permanently. If we obey God this will be a fact. We need to work together with His Spirit and walk with God.

In chapter five of the epistle John says, **"By this we know that we love the children of God, when we love God and observe His commandments.** (1 John 5:2). When we are abiding, that is, obeying we can know that we have a love for the brethren. When we are loving God we will show our love for them. John also brings up the point of how we can know we love God. He says, **"For this is the love of God, that we keep His commandments; and His commandments are not burdensome"** (1 John 5:3). Jesus said, **"My yoke is easy, and My burden is light"** (Matthew 11:30). God's commands are not burdensome if we are walking in the Spirit. When we are living for the Lord we see that God's commands are the way of true life, the abundant life. Let me point out that again we see obedience as of utmost importance. We can only confidently say we love God when we are walking in His commandments. Many sing out that they love God, but do they really love Him?

Several verses later John will write, **"These things I have written to you who believe in the name of the Son of God, so that you may know that you have eternal life"** (1 John 5:13). How can we really know we have eternal life? By a prayer we prayed years ago, or a baptismal ceremony we went through? By how often we get to church, or how much we give? No. We can only really know that we have eternal life if we are walking in obedience to God, abiding in Christ. Obeying the commands of God is of utmost importance for those who say they love Him. Let's obey.

Chapter 13
A Look At Second & Third John

As we begin our look at Second John the   apostle continues to talk about obedience in the Christian life. He writes, **"I was very glad to find *some* of your children walking in truth, just as we have received commandment *to do* from the Father"** (2 John 1:4). I cannot emphasize enough that God didn't save us primarily to go to heaven; He saved us to live transformed lives, to be like Jesus, and this *only* happens through the obedience of faith.

Love is the supreme action of our life in Christ, but what is love? John says, **"And this is love, that we walk according to His commandments"** (2 John 1:6a). You just can't get away from obedience when it comes to true Christianity! Whether it is love of the brethren, or love for God, it is based in a holy life—an obedient life. John continues in the same verse saying, **"This is the commandment, just as you have heard from the beginning, that you should walk in it"** (2 John 1:6b). To truly fulfill the commandment to love we need walk in obedience to the commands of God.

We can do loving things without love. If that doesn't make any sense then consider what the apostle Paul said in 1 Corinthians 13:3: **"If I give all my possessions to feed *the poor*, and if I surrender my body to be burned, but do not have love, it profits me nothing."** These are very loving things, yet, in this case, they were done without love at all. We need to walk in obedience and then our loving actions will truly be out of love.

A couple of verses later John will present a very interesting statement. He writes, **"Watch yourselves, that you do not lose what we have accomplished,** (2 John 1:8a). It would seem that the heights and rewards that we attain to can disappear on us. He goes on to say, **"but that you may receive a full reward"** (2 John 1:8b). He doesn't specify here how we can lose out, but he has often been talking about obedience, so I would conclude that we lose out through disobedience. He isn't talking here about missing out on glory, but of the rewards in glory.

In the very next verse he says, **"Anyone who goes too far and does not abide in the teaching of Christ, does not have God"** (2 John 1:9a). John has been talking about obedience and love. He says here that if we go out of these teachings, or beyond them, we do **"not have God."** We need to be students of the Word so we know the truth. John goes on to say, **"The one who abides in the teaching, he has both the Father and the Son"** (2 John 1:9b). Let's stay in the teachings, both theologically and by practical living.

As we begin our look at Third John we find him saying, **"For I was very glad when brethren came and testified to your truth,** *that is,* **how you are walking in truth.** (3 John 1:3). Are you living the Word of God? If so then people will hear of it and they will rejoice. He adds, **"I have no greater joy than this, to hear of my children walking in the truth."** (3 John 1:4). Is obedience in the Christian life important? Oh, yes. Is it important to you like it was to John? He found no greater joy than to see Christians obeying God with their lives.

A number of verses later John writes, **"Beloved, do not imitate what is evil, but what is good"** (3 John 1:11). I have to admit that for so many years I imitated the evil practices of the world. I hope that is not your situation. We are rather to copy what is good, and godly. John goes on to say, **"The one who does good is of God; the one who does evil has not seen God"** (3 John 1:11). We can be church goers for years and not really see God. If this is the case we need to repent and come to Christ, seeking Him in obedience. How do we know for sure we know God? By living for Him. That is the only way.

Chapter 14
A Look At Jude

As we begin our look at Jude we will look at his reason for writing the epistle:

Beloved, while I was making every effort to write you about our common salvation, I felt the necessity to write to you appealing that you contend earnestly for the faith which was once for all handed down to the saints. ⁴ For certain persons have crept in unnoticed, those who were long beforehand marked out for this condemnation, ungodly persons who turn the grace of our God into licentiousness and deny our only Master and Lord, Jesus Christ. (Jude 1:3-4)

He says that originally he was going to write about **"our common salvation."** That is what Paul wrote about in Ephesians. However, he **"felt the necessity"** to write about some terrible things that were going on in their midst. On the basis of this he appealed to them that they would **"contend earnestly for the faith"** (Jude 1:3b). This is what we need to do today, and it is the reason I have written this series of books.

Jude says that men have slipped into the church and they are not true Christians. They are **"ungodly persons who turn the grace of our God into licentiousness"** (Jude 1:4b). These men, no matter what they profess, are godless; we can see this by their lifestyle. As is often the case, they are involved in sexual sin—deeply involved. Jude says they take advantage of God's grace by suggesting it covers their debauchery. They say, "Hey, we're saved by God's grace!" In doing this they **"deny our only Master and Lord, Jesus Christ"** (Jude 1:4c). Jesus is not to be merely Savior of the Christian, but Master *and* Lord.

Jude has an interesting statement near the end of the short epistle. He says, **"Keep yourselves in the love of God, waiting anxiously for the mercy of our Lord Jesus Christ to eternal life"** (Jude 1:21). What does he mean by **"Keep yourselves in the love of God"**? Well, part of it is **"waiting anxiously for the mercy of our Lord Jesus Christ."** We need to have our eye on the prize. To do this we need to walk in obedience. This is consistent with his purpose in writing—**"appealing that you contend earnestly for the faith."** We keep ourselves in God's love by obedience, or as John put it, abiding in Christ.

In his next to last verse Jude writes, **"Now to Him who is able to keep you from stumbling, and to make you stand in the presence of His glory blameless with great joy."** (Jude 1:24). Praise and glory to God Jesus is able to keep us from stumbling; but we can keep this from happening through sin. He can't keep us from stumbling if we don't seek Him, that is, abide in Him. For those who seek Him, turning from sin and the world, Jesus will make them stand firm; they will be blameless before God and have the greatest joy. What a contrast from those who John speaks of in 1 John 2:28 who have to shrink away from Christ at His return. Let's walk in obedience, brothers and sisters.

Chapter 15
A Look At Revelation
(Part one)

As we begin a look at Revelation we will start with the words of the glorified Lord Jesus to the church at Ephesus. He says, **"But I have *this* against you, that you have left your first love"** (Revelation 2:4). Most of us would agree that their first love was the Lord Jesus Himself. They started out well with Paul starting the church and working among them on and off for many years. Yet while starting strong and still doing some things quite well as Jesus points out to them, they had turned from their love of Jesus. Imagine a church that does not love Jesus first and foremost. I'm sure it happens more than we think.

Jesus said, **"Therefore remember from where you have fallen"** (Revelation 2:5a). They were to think back and remember the heights they had attained. How was it shown that they had fallen? By their lack of obedience. It was said to them, **"repent and do the deeds you did at first; or else I am coming to you and will remove your lampstand out of its place—unless you repent."** (Revelation 2:4-5). If you look back on your early days do you still see the same zeal and obedience? If not then, like the Ephesians, you need to repent and **"do the deeds you did at first."**

Jesus continued a couple of verses later by saying, **"He who has an ear, let him hear what the Spirit says to the churches. To him who overcomes, I will grant to eat of the tree of life which is in the Paradise of God"** (Revelation 2:7). Some think it was just the churches spoken to who needed to overcome in the Christian life; as if because it is written in Revelation it is somehow different. Well, the church existed in the book of Acts. If they needed to overcome to **"eat of the tree of life"** then we need to do so as well.

To the church at Smyrna Jesus said, **"Do not fear what you are about to suffer. Behold, the devil is about to cast some of you into prison, so that you will be tested, and you will have tribulation for ten days"** (Revelation 2:10a). Great trouble from Satan was coming upon them to test them. What did they need to do? They needed to be obedient to God through it. Jesus said, **"Be faithful until death, and I will give you the crown of life"** (Revelation 2:10b). Again, these were Christians just like you and me, living in the Church Age just like you and me. If they needed to be faithful to death then we do as well. If we do so Jesus will give us **"the crown of life."** Jesus continues, **"He who has an ear, let him hear what the Spirit says to the churches. He who overcomes will not be hurt by the second death."** (Revelation 2:11). The Lake of Fire is the second death; if we are overcomers against sin we will not experience the Lake of Fire.

To the church at Pergamum Jesus said, **"He who has an ear, let him hear what the Spirit says to the churches. To him who overcomes, to him I will give *some* of the hidden manna, and I will give him a white stone, and a new name written on the stone which no one knows but he who receives it"** (Revelation 2:17). Again, we see that we need to overcome in the Christian life; it is not a matter of merely praying the sinner's prayer. We need to hear what the Spirit says, and we need to walk in the power of the Spirit of God.

A few verses later Jesus is talking about a woman named Jezebel who was leading the brethren away from Christ. Jesus said in verse twenty-one that He even gave her **"time to repent."** This shows the forbearance of God, yet it also shows that it comes to an end if there is no repentance. He goes on and says, **"And I will kill her children with pestilence, and all the churches will know that I am He who searches the minds and hearts; and I will give to each one of you according to your deeds"** (Revelation 2:23). Whether it is a false teacher like Jezebel or it is a true Christian we will be judged according to our deeds whether good or bad (2 Corinthians 5:10).

Chapter 16
A Look At Revelation
(Part two)

To the church at Thyatira Jesus said, **"Nevertheless what you have, hold fast until I come.** (Revelation 2:25). Whether it was a believer in the Bible or us, we need to **"hold fast"** until Jesus returns. We need to walk in obedience. Jesus continued saying, **"He who overcomes, and he who keeps My deeds until the end, to him I will give authority over the nations"** (Revelation 2:26). Do we want heavenly blessings, in this case authority over the nations, then we need to keep Jesus' deeds **"until the end."**

The church at Sardis had fallen asleep at the wheel. Jesus said to them, **"Wake up, and strengthen the things that remain, which were about to die; for I have not found your deeds completed in the sight of My God"** (Revelation 3:2). If Jesus were to look over your life, which He does, would He find your deeds complete? I hope so. He continues a couple of verses later by saying, **"He who overcomes will thus be clothed in white garments; and I will not erase his name from the book of life, and I will confess his name before My Father and before His angels"** (Revelation 3:5). To the one who overcomes in the Christian life Jesus will cloth them in white garments—garments of righteousness. Also, He will **"not erase his name from the book of life."** Apparently, our names can be erased! Most people teach this can't happen, but Jesus wouldn't have brought it up if it weren't a possibility. We need to fear and walk in His will. Jesus adds, **"I will confess his name before My Father and before His angels."** We certainly want Jesus to speak well of us and our lives before the Father. We need to obey God.

To the church at Philadelphia Jesus said, **"I am coming quickly; hold fast what you have, so that no one will take your crown.** (Revelation 3:11). Jesus could return at any moment. We need to **"hold fast what [we] have."** We can't just begin the Christian life strong; we need to finish strong as well. Jesus said we need to be careful that **"no one will take your crown."** I think the crown represents rewards. We cannot shrink back in disobedience or our rewards will be taken away by the sin we are in.

He continues, **"He who overcomes, I will make him a pillar in the temple of My God, and he will not go out from it anymore"** (Revelation 3:12a). In all these messages Jesus talks about overcoming a lot; it is obviously very important. The Christian life is more than attending church on Sunday mornings. If we overcome Jesus will make us a **"pillar in the temple of My God."** Pillars in that day were not only very prominent, but were very important as well. Jesus says, **"and I will write on him the name of My God, and the name of the city of My God, the new Jerusalem, which comes down out of heaven from My God, and My new name"** (Revelation 3:12b). If we want these things to be a part of our futures we need to endure.

To the church at Laodicea Jesus gave a message that is very well known to all of us. He said, **"Behold, I stand at the door and knock; if anyone hears My voice and opens the door, I will come in to him and will dine with him, and he with Me"** (Revelation 3:20). Usually these words are used for the unbelieving as an invitation to come to Christ for salvation, but notice it is spoken to believers. Jesus is not in their hearts apparently. In their pursuit of sin they threw Him out. He was left to knock on the door, hoping for an invitation in. Jesus wants to be at home in our hearts and then He will fellowship with us, and we with Him. Jesus continues, **"He who overcomes, I will grant to him to sit down with Me on My throne, as I also overcame and sat down with My Father on His throne"** (Revelation 3:21). Again, Jesus tells the believers that they need to overcome in the Christian life. We all have temptations and troubles, and we all need to be conquers in these things.

Chapter 17
A Look At Revelation
(Part three)

As we continue our look at Revelation as you would expect we will be confronted with some symbolism. John writes, **"So the dragon was enraged with the woman, and went off to make war with the rest of her children, who keep the commandments of God and hold to the testimony of Jesus"** (Revelation 12:17). The dragon is of course Satan; the woman, as I understand it, represents Israel. **"The rest of her children"** represent believing Jews or perhaps non-Jewish believers. Either way, they are those **"who keep the commandments of God and hold to the testimony of Jesus."** This is what we who live today are called to do. We are to be obedient to the commands of God, and stand firm on the testimony of a righteous life—the testimony of Jesus. He always obeyed the Father and we are called to do the same.

As we get into chapter fourteen John is talking about those who do not follow God, and receive the mark of the Beast. Then John says, **"Here is the perseverance of the saints who keep the commandments of God and their faith in Jesus"** (Revelation 14:12). In those days believers will need to persevere. Is it any different today? Absolutely not. We won't go through the same trials as they will, but we need to be faithful to the end as they will need to. Next John writes, **"And I heard a voice from heaven, saying, 'Write, "Blessed are the dead who die in the Lord from now on!"' 'Yes,' says the Spirit, 'so that they may rest from their labors, for their deeds follow with them.'"** (Revelation 14:13). Just as their deeds will follow them so will ours. You and I need to walk in obedience of the commands of God.

As we continue we will find John talking about believers being the bride of Christ. He says this, **"It was given to her to clothe herself in fine linen, bright *and* clean"** (Revelation 19:8a). It is fine linen which is bright and clean, but what is this clothing? John tells us, **"For the fine linen is the righteous acts of the saints"** (Revelation 19:8b). Believe it or not the fine clothing is our good deeds! Amazing! What kind of materiel are we offering up to the Lord by our choices?

Later John will be talking about the new earth, and God saying, **"He who overcomes will inherit these things, and I will be his God and he will be My son"** (Revelation 21:7). Do God's standards change? Is He going to make those people overcome to inherit the new earth, but let us slide? I think you will agree that this is not the case. God's standards are the same for all of us—faithful obedience.

The last verse we will look at is from the last chapter of Revelation. We find the glorified Lord Jesus talking, and He says, **"Behold, I am coming quickly, and My reward *is* with Me, to render to every man according to what he has done"** (Revelation 22:12). Jesus' reward for believers who persevere is with Him; notice that He says He will **"render to every man according to what he has done."** What is it that you have done? Good or bad we will be called to account. May we repent if necessary, and follow the King of Kings.

Chapter 18
Closing Words

James writes what are some of the most important words of all the epistles, **"But prove yourselves doers of the word"** (James 1:22a). Indeed, we need to put the promises of God, and the commands of God into practice. When God's Word says set aside filthiness, we need to do so. When God's Word says don't worry, we've got to stop worrying. We need to be practitioners of the Word **"and not merely hearers who delude themselves"** (James 1:22b). When we take in the Bible on Sunday mornings or during our own study time, and we don't take obedient action we merely **"delude"** ourselves into thinking we are virtuous. Many think just being at the Bible study, or at church is the goal. It merely begins there.

In James 2:20 he writes, **"But are you willing to recognize, you foolish fellow, that faith without works is useless?"** It is interesting that James refers to those who call themselves Christians, but have no change in their lives, **"foolish."** It is foolhardy to expect to stand before the infinitely holy God of all Creation with a faith that couldn't produce any transformation. He says a faith without godly works is **"useless."** Jesus talked about the same thing when He said, **"You are the salt of the earth; but if the salt has become tasteless, how can it be made salty *again*? It is no longer good for anything, except to be thrown out and trampled underfoot by men"** (Matthew 5:13).

Peter talked about those who wanted the best out of life. He wrote, **"He must turn away from evil and do good; he must seek peace and pursue it"** (1 Peter 3:11a). We are seeing that if we want the best out of life Peter says we need to obey; we need to pursue peace with God and with our fellow man. Why? **"For the eyes of the Lord are toward the righteous, and His ears attend to their prayer"** (1 Peter 3:12a). If we turn from evil God will look lovingly upon us, and He will here our prayers. Many think God just hears our prayers because we are Christians, but that doesn't seem to be the case. Peter goes on and says, **"But the face of the Lord is against those who do evil."** (1 Peter 3:12b). Remember, this was written for Christians, not the unbelieving. If we have turned from the Lord and walk in disobedience God turns His face from us. How sad for us.

Peter talked about adding a number of qualities to our lives. Then he said, **"For if these *qualities* are yours and are increasing, they render you neither useless nor unfruitful in the true knowledge of our Lord Jesus Christ"** (2 Peter 1:8). We need to add these qualities and grow in them or we will be **"useless nor unfruitful"** in God's hands. Peter wanted to pound this point home so he added, **"For he who lacks these *qualities* is blind *or* short-sighted,   having forgotten *his* purification from his former sins"** (2 Peter 1:9). **"Blind *or* short-sighted;"** I think the blind are those who are in deep sin in their lives, and those who are short-sighted are true believers who have fallen asleep at the wheel. He is talking about true believers because he says it is this person who has **"forgotten *his* purification from his former sins."**

Peter goes on to say, **"Therefore, brethren, be all the more diligent to make certain about His calling and choosing you"** (2 Peter 1:10a). This is interesting. We are to be **"all the more diligent"** to make certain that we are saved! That is what he says: **"make certain about His calling**

and choosing you." How do we make certain we are saved? By the fact that we prayed a prayer years ago? No. By obedience; by adding those things he listed to our faith and continually growing in them.

John said, **"But if we walk in the Light as He Himself is in the Light, we have fellowship with one another"** (1 John 1:7a). If we turn from sin we will have true fellowship with other Christians who are doing likewise. This isn't talking about being sinless, though that is our goal, but living honestly before God. John says if we do this **"the blood of Jesus His Son cleanses us from all sin"** (1 John 1:7b). Most of us thought the blood of Christ did all its work at the cross, but in reality it is still doing its work. John continues, **"If we confess our sins, He is faithful and righteous to forgive us our sins and to cleanse us from all unrighteousness"** (1 John 1:9). Still, after conversion, we need the blood of Christ; we still need forgiveness. I had been lead to believe all my sins (past, present, and future) were forgiven at the time of conversion. That doesn't appear true. It would seem that if we don't confess our sins we will not be forgiven for sins we commit.

Jude has an interesting statement near the end of the short epistle. He says, **"Keep yourselves in the love of God, waiting anxiously for the mercy of our Lord Jesus Christ to eternal life"** (Jude 1:21). What does he mean by **"Keep yourselves in the love of God"**? Well, part of it is **"waiting anxiously for the mercy of our Lord Jesus Christ."** We need to have our eye on the prize. To do this we need to walk in obedience. This is consistent with his purpose in writing— **"appealing that you contend earnestly for the faith."** We keep ourselves in God's love by obedience, or as John put it, abiding in Christ.

To the church at Laodicea Jesus gave a message that is very well known to all of us. He said, **"Behold, I stand at the door and knock; if anyone hears My voice and opens the door, I will come in to him and will dine with him, and he with Me"** (Revelation 3:20). Usually these words are used for the unbelieving as an invitation to come to Christ for salvation, but notice it is spoken to believers. Jesus is not in their hearts apparently. In their pursuit of sin they threw Him out. He was left to knock on the door, hoping for an invitation in. Jesus wants to be at home in our hearts and then He will fellowship with us, and we with Him. Jesus continues, **"He who overcomes, I will grant to him to sit down with Me on My throne, as I also overcame and sat down with My Father on His throne"** (Revelation 3:21). Again, Jesus tells the believers that they need to overcome in the Christian life. We all have temptations and troubles, and we all need to be conquers in these things.

We have finished our look at James through Revelation. I hope it has been a help to you as you seek the Lord. Glory to His Name!

About the Author

I am identifying myself only as brother Jon, because I love when a brother or sister in Christ calls me brother Jon, or just brother. In an instant it reminds me that I am in Christ, and that we are in this together. May we help one another to fight the good fight of faith. Also, and more importantly, our focus should not be on who promoted this or who wrote that. It should be upon our Glorious and Wonderful God, our Father in Heaven, and on His Marvelous Son, our Savior, Christ Jesus. *Jesus is Lord!*

Remember the prisoners, as though in prison with them, *and* those who are ill-treated, since you yourselves also are in the body.
Hebrews 13:13

Books included in *The Ten Series*:

Ephesians
Philippians
Colossians
2 Thessalonians
2 Timothy
Titus
James
1 Peter
2 Peter
Jude

Books included in *The Doers Of The Word series*:

The Obedience Of Faith (Acts-Colossians)
The Obedience Of Faith (1Thessalonians-Hebrews)
The Obedience Of Faith (James-Revelation)
The Obedience Of Faith (Acts-Revelation)

Following are other titles written by Brother Jon:

*(All of them are available on Amazon or through
your local bookstore)*

Fellowship Prayer

The Missing Foundation

This was my first book and indeed the most foundational; in it I seek to show that most of us devote so little time to prayer that we spend our time petitioning God to the exclusion of fellowshipping with Him. I show that, in complete contrast to this, Jesus spent great amounts of time in prayer. Please consider Mark 1:35, **"In the early morning, while it was still dark, Jesus got up, left *the house*, and went away to a secluded place, and was praying there."** Now, the verse clearly does not say He spent *every* morning doing this, but that particular morning He did; however, we would probably be foolish to think this was the only morning He got up early to pray. I, for one, am fully convinced that this was His regular habit.

I have no proof, no verse to point to, but I find it hard to imagine that Jesus got up early in the morning to run off dozens of petitions to the exclusion of spending quality one-on-one time with the Father. I am convinced that the foundation of Jesus' prayer life was fellowship with the Father, with our God and His God. *I am also convinced that this, fellowship prayer, is the missing foundation of the prayer life of many Christians.*

Most Christians spend virtually all of their prayer time in petitioning God for themselves and others. *Praying for others and ourselves is a marvelous gift, but I don't think that it is designed to be the heart of our prayer lives.* Very little if any time is spent truly focused on the Great and Mighty God that we are petitioning, and with this book I want to help change that.

If you want to be a real man or woman of God you *must* make fellowship prayer a strong foundation of your life.

Fellowship Living: The Abundant Life

We live our lives day after day with a multitude of different thoughts traveling through our minds. We daydream about the future, or about this silliness or that. We replay and replay again a conversation or situation that took place a few minutes earlier. It can even be from days, weeks, or even years earlier. The truth is we are more like the fictional Walter Mitty than the one we call Lord and Savior.

We are told by the Lord Jesus to love God with all our minds, but we almost constantly entertain whatever happens to be playing on the cinema of our minds. Oh, we generally put out the filthy stuff, and the evil thoughts are put out too, but what about the rest? Paul said to take every thought captive, and we are nowhere near doing this.

I will present the case that we need to have prayer lives that are filled to overflowing with praise and worship of our great God, rather than overflowing with requests. I call this Fellowship Prayer. We then need to continue the worship as we go into and through our daily lives. I call this Fellowship Living. This combination will indeed produce the abundant life that Jesus came to give. It won't just produce it, it is the abundant life!

The Sun Has No Light
When Compared To Your Glory, Oh God

The Sun has no light when compared to your glory, Oh God! As they say, truer words were never spoken. Using my very limited and unworthy ability, I will seek to communicate a picture in words of Our Great God, the God of the Bible. I will seek to show that He is the most breathtakingly Marvelous Being, and all praise is do His Glorious Name!

I begin with a unique look at God from the Scriptures. Understanding through the Word that He is more personal and intimately involved than we have seen. I show how He very much wants to be personally involved in each of our lives. From there I go into a section of the creation itself, pointing out in very practical ways how magnificent our God is.

In the last section I show that we have greatly fallen short and have remade Christianity into religious expression rather than a genuinely personal communion with the Creator. I also call the reader to the foundation of that relationship which is Fellowship Prayer. I show that Jesus made this the foundation of His life, and we need to as well.

Man's Duty
In Light Of God's Sovereignty

If we had a view of God that was millions of times greater than we have, God would still be infinitely grander than that. Our God is most awesome, and that is what I want to show in the first one-third of this short book. God is most awesome, and He is the Sovereign One. From there I will go into our responsibility in light of His Sovereignty and grace. The last third of the book will cover the duty of man in light of what is generally understood in terms of predestination.

God partnered with mankind to care for the earth and its creatures. God partners with parents to raise their children properly. God partners with governments to bring about justice and foster the goodness of life. So too God partners with individuals and churches to bring to fruition the salvation that is only available in Christ our Savior.

We have a part to play. We cannot continue to love our own lives and the things of this world as we wait for Heaven. The Apostle Paul said, "So then, my beloved, just as you have always obeyed, not as in my presence only, but now much more in my absence, work out your salvation with fear and trembling; 13 for it is God who is at work in you, both to will and to work for His good pleasure" (Philippians 2:12-13).

These two verses are my whole point, and there is no other.

Partnership Salvation

I think we have viewed salvation the wrong way. As I have understood over the years there are two basic views. One, is that it is all the work of God, and we merely exercise faith to enter. It is immediately a finished work—Heaven awaits, come Hell or high water, or complete sinfulness and foolishness on our part. In the end it doesn't matter because we've been saved by God's grace. The other view is that we can lose our salvation through sinful living, and I suppose false teaching. I have a third view, and I will endeavor to lay out the Scriptures so you can see it as well.

I spend as much time in Fellowship Prayer as I can, and one day while doing just that, these words were brought to my mind, *"Salvation is a partnership."* I understand this statement, salvation is a partnership, to mean that Jesus saves, and we remain in Him through obedient action.

We will see from both Mathew and John that Jesus taught this. That should be enough, but I will show from seven New Testament books that this is what the Bible teaches. I certainly did not set out to present what could be seen as a compromise between the "once saved always saved" crowd, and those who teach that "you can lose your salvation," but in essence that is what I have done. While in one sense it is a compromise of these two views, and holds similarities to both of them, it is completely different from both of them. You would have to abandon them to embrace what I will be showing you. I hope you take the time to humbly consider what I will be presenting.

The Day
Of
JUDGMENT

Let me just say right away, that I understand that there are two judgments, one for Believers and one for unbelievers, and these will take place at two different times. The Lord Jesus spoke of them as one event and I will do the same. I will touch on the Great White Throne Judgment, but I will be speaking almost exclusively of the believer's judgment.

The judgment will be huge in its scale, and it will also be huge in its importance. I am of the belief that most Christians view the judgment more or less as a "speed bump" as we proceed into glory. Yes, I am of the impression that most see it as though it were virtually meaningless. If God allows I hope to help change that.

Maybe I'm cynical, but I am convinced that most Christians are pretty much focused on this world, and somewhere off in the distance, out of the corner of their eye they see Eternity. When on the relatively rare occasion they look ahead to Eternity they see little more than Heavenly glory. The coming judgment, that was very important to the Lord Jesus, is hardly even noticed.

I am convinced that when we look ahead to the eternal that the judgment might be something that should be catching our eye. Until recently I saw the judgment as something very private, very small, and very quick. That is the complete opposite of how I view it now, and I am hope is the opposite of how you will view it after reading these pages.

From The Holy Bible:
How Christians Should View
The Catholic Church

Some time ago I had become very interested in learning more about the Catholic Church because the Church seemed more than okay to many Christians; they saw it as being quite good, and considered it as just a "different flavor" of Christianity. So I purchased a newly released and very thick book that had been written under the direction of the Pope. The book was entitled *Catechism of the Catholic Church* and it contained the official doctrines of the Church.

In this official book of Catholic doctrine I found what I was looking for and I began a long, and diligent study of their major teachings. I ended up condensing the book's eight hundred and three pages down to six pages, focusing on six of the most important teachings of the Catholic Church. I compared these doctrines with associated teachings from the Bible, and this is what I have presented in this very short book.

If you do not want to face the truth of the false teachings of the Catholic Church, and you do not want to face the reality that we need to boldly tell Catholics that they need to abandon the false religion they have embraced their whole lives, and in repentance turn to the true Jesus of the Bible, then do not read this short book.

The following are evangelistic books under the author Jon Brothers:

Consider The World In Which We Live

I have been noticing clouds lately. Noting their formations, density, height and things. I had never paid much attention before. Oh, I'd certainly noticed them and on a few occasions over the years stopped what I was doing and stood in awe at the sight, but now I seem to be in awe of them daily. While walking at the park recently I passed some trees and looked up to my right and there was a cloud, small but with some body to it. I noticed it was lumbering slowly along. Then I noticed smaller clouds beyond it. Wisps of clouds, actually. After a moment I noticed they were traveling along too, but in almost the opposite direction.

Then I thought about the breeze that had been cooling me while I was walking—it was coming from a third direction! I had never really thought about it, but I suppose I had assumed all wind traveled in the same direction. The wind, however, was traveling in at least three different directions.

I hope you will join me and look through these few pages as I talk about the world around us. We will take a brief, layman's look at things we see daily as we go about our lives, and we will also consider some things that most of us only see in pictures. The world around us is quite amazing; however, we are often too busy living our lives to notice it. I would like to help you see things differently, very differently.

Everything Has A Designer

There are countless things around us, and all of them were created by someone or a group of people. Every moment of our lives we are standing or sitting on something that was designed. If we can look at these things and recognize there is a designer and they didn't come about by chance, so we have got to see it in ourselves and the world around us.

Made in the USA
Coppell, TX
17 March 2021